A New Taxonomy:
The seven law firm business models

BRUCE MACEWEN

Adam Smith, Esq.®
New York
2014

ALSO BY BRUCE MACEWEN

GROWTH IS DEAD: NOW WHAT?

LAW FIRMS ON THE BRINK (2013)

Published by Adam Smith, Esq., LLC
305 West 98th Street
New York, New York 10025
USA

*Library of Congress Cataloging-in-Publication Data is
available*
ISBN 978-0615914190

Composed and published at New York, New York.

Printed in the United States of America

Cover design and graphics by faucethead creative

Contents

Foreword by David Morley

I run a big law firm - Allen & Overy. Widely known as A&O. I've been lucky enough to be at the firm 33 years. A partner for 25 of those years. Unimaginative, perhaps. Unchanging or unchallenging, never.

I've seen it grow from 35 partners when I joined to 529 partners today. I've seen it expand from one office in one country to 42 offices in 29 countries. I've been in charge in good times and bad. I was in charge when Lehman went under.

If I've learned anything, it's the importance of context. Lawyers are often rightly accused of not seeing the wood for the trees. Of paying inordinate attention to detail. Whilst the devil can be in the detail, the best lawyers also put things into context. They keep things in perspective. They see the bigger picture.

My test of a good business book is simple: does it provide context that clarifies your thinking? This book does. It's a good one.

Don't be put off by the title. It may sound technical, dull even. It's anything but. It paints the BigLaw order of battle for seven different law firm models in vivid colours on a broad canvas. It helps you see the whole battlefield, not just the skirmishes.

When you first meet Bruce, three things will happen.

First, you look upwards. I'm 6'2" but I still had to look upwards. As you do, you take in a spare, well dressed figure.

Secondly, you are charmed. By his generosity of spirit and old world politeness.

Thirdly, you are tested - his mildly whimsical style cloaks a deep interest in - using his phrases, 'Law Land' and 'BigLaw' - that sets you thinking. Any easy business assumptions or woolly strategic thinking you've allowed yourself will be gently but relentlessly exposed.

Bruce is an author of immense experience. As a lawyer, in house and in private practice. As a consultant to law firms. As a commentator and author of over 1500 articles on the business of law. He's also founder of renowned legal web site Adam Smith, Esq. (I know a legal website is renown when my partners start sending me links to articles in it with accompanying messages to the effect that: "This is so true!" or "Were you aware of this?").

He's written for such august publications as the *Wall Street Journal* and *The New York Times* as well as trade publications like *The National Law Journal*, *The Lawyer* and *Legal Week*. All that experience gives him an elegance of style and economy of expression which makes your thoughts flow through the 100 pages.

His mission is clear. Compile a guide to law firm business models. Identify law firm 'species'. Provide a conceptual map to the industry.

Why?

Because almost everyone who matters now realises BigLaw is changing at a rate never seen in our lifetimes. Never, he rightly says, has the future seemed "as shrouded in fog and noise". This book will help the fog to clear a little. Enough to see where you are. Enough to see more clearly where you might go.

In some ways Bruce is more Joseph Schumpeter than Adam Smith. Schumpeter once said: "Economic progress, in capitalist society, means turmoil". Bruce sees Darwinian evolutionary and market forces bearing down on law firms. Firms must adapt or risk withering away. Far from being a bad thing, he sees this as entirely welcome and long overdue - "we need the equivalent of a Cambrian Explosion in Law Land" he says.

Yet he's not unsympathetic to the stresses and strains. The human cost. He's not blind to the potential damage to long standing customs and firm cultures. He's not oblivious to the economic upheaval. It's just that he sees change as inevitable. He sees opportunities for firms that can unite. That can deploy character as well as intellect. He sees a better world emerging.

It's that ultimately hopeful, positive vision of the future of Law Land that should compel you to read this book. These are not the writings of a doom monger or naysayer intent on predicting Armageddon. These are the writings of a liberal mind. Curious and excited about the possibilities for the future. Urging his readers to prepare for battle. Gird their loins. To face forward, not backward.

> David Morley is the worldwide Senior Partner
> of Allen & Overy and is based in London

The good things of prosperity are to be wished;
but the good things that belong to adversity are to be
admired.

— Seneca (4 BC—AD 65)

Introduction to the taxonomy

We humans like to put things in categories.

And while we can get it plain wrong, or mix up two categories benignly or malignly, there's no question our propensity for categorization—from friend or foe and food to poison, to Linnaeus, to the periodic table, to the Dewey decimal system—has gotten us a long way on the planet so far.

So we launch our own conceptual map, or taxonomy, of law firms.

The ground rules:

- We're only categorizing BigLaw, or Sophisticated Law; but you knew that.
- Do not make the flat out wrong assumption that any of these models requires or entails a one-size-fits-all approach to quality, pricing, profitability, or anything else. Many firms following the same model can have extremely different approaches to where they fit on the prestige scale, where their clientele primarily comes from, the caliber of talent they attract and require, and so forth. In short, you can serve the top, the middle, or the value portion of the market under any of these models.
- We are not going to identify firms by name who fit into any specific category; you can play that game at home. (Actually, we did ask you for

your opinions in an online poll and we show you the results in Chapter 9.)

- Membership in a particular category for a particular firm is not static; firms can, have, and will continue to, move between categories. In fact, we live for and celebrate dynamism.

So without further ado:

The Models
Global Players spanning three or more continents
Capital Markets centric firms headquartered in a global financial center—often historically tethered to a major investment bank
Kings of Their Hill firms headquartered in non-global cities catering to sophisticated upper and middle market, mostly non-financial services companies, and very high net worth individuals
Boutiques known *primarily* for one thing
Category Killer specialists targeting one broad but not necessarily high-intrinsic-value practice
The Hollow Middle One-size-fits-all, not a special destination, generic law firms
Integrated Focus firms, a newly emergent species[1]

---

[1] In the version of the taxonomy that appeared on Adam Smith, Esq. online, these firms were called "synergistic super-boutiques." As screenwriters say, "only the name has been changed." Why? First, because "synergistic" has been so grossly overused as to suck all meaning out of it; and second, because using the word "boutique"

I believe an analogy to biological classification is useful in understanding the ecosystem of law firms because there's competition within species (between individual firms who are essentially alike) as well as competition across species (between, e.g., global firms and boutiques). There's also, as we know well, the phenomena of birth, death and perhaps even extinction of certain categories. [2]

Each of the next chapters will discuss the pro's and con's, challenges and opportunities, facing each particular model, as well as what the management priorities for that type of firm ought to be.

A continuous theme that drives the narrative and the analysis of this work is that while, as we will see, each

twice in one taxonomy seemed a dubious call. (We continually reserve the right to change our mind.)

[2] The complete biological classification system is far more hierarchical and detailed than our one-dimensional conceptual map. For example, the complete Linnaean taxonomy for human beings reads down thus:

- domain/eukarya
- kingdom/animalia
- phylum/chordata
- class/mammalia
- order/primates
- family/hominidae
- genus/homo
- species/sapien

category has intrinsic strengths and vulnerabilities, individual firms can grow and/or thrive, or shrivel and/or fail, in every single category.

Slipping your firm neatly into any particular category will by no means assure your prosperity or doom you to a marginalized future. In plain English, every category is populated both with smart, savvy, agile firms, and with obtuse, complacent, and self-satisfied firms.

In a "growth is dead" world, where the salient feature of our competitive battlefield is that we are fighting over market share, management by autopilot—and management by reflexively seeking out the comfort zone of the tried and true—will fail to distinguish your firm in the eyes of your clients. Undistinguished is hard to separate from unimpressive, and unimpressive quickly ripens into irrelevant.

Conversely, firms that are unblinkingly realistic about knowing who they are, and who play to their strengths, choosing their fights prudently, will stand out and be rewarded for it.

In short, clarity of vision and resolve in leadership matter as never before. Whatever category you're in.

GLOBAL PLAYERS

Global Players

Global players are where everyone seemed to want to be only a few short years ago, so it's only fitting we start with them.

Let's get to it.

First, let's define our terms: By "global players," I mean firms spanning three or more continents, top of the food chain predators but, like predators, limited in number.

Pros

- Presence everywhere that matters
- Have created their own barrier to entry
- Comprehensive practice area offerings
- Areas of very high intrinsic profitability
- Sheer scale may enable firms to make greater investments in firm-wide resources such as IT and training, as the costs will be spread over a wider base
- Finally, these firms have widespread brand awareness, simply from their ubiquity

Cons

By and large, there are no economies of scale in law firms, using that phrase in the strict economic sense of decreasing unit costs of production solely due to greater size

- Marginal offices, with continuing churn of openings and closings around the periphery
- Specific practice areas and sectors can suffer cycles of flaccid demand
- Risk of a pachyderm-like lack of responsiveness
- Compensation across a very wide network with areas of high and low intrinsic profitability and high and low costs of living can be a big headache

Management priorities

- Try to remain nimble in maintaining an economically compelling geographic footprint and practice area mix
- Stay on top of enormous managerial complexity and overhead
- Maintain and reinforce the core concept of a "one-firm firm" across time zones, cultures, languages, and more.

What else can we say about global players?

Some of the earliest—Coudert Bros., e.g.—are no longer with us, and others have failed to live up to their potential; this is a back-door way of

> We bandy about the term "one-firm firm" fairly promiscuously, but with global players it really has teeth.

saying this business model, which everybody and their brother seemingly used to aspire to, is no panacea.

Second, the burden of managerial complexity needs to be called out for special attention. I know managing partners of some of these firms who live on airplanes. That's glamorous for about a month, and then it quickly becomes a long-run endurance test of one's physical constitution, dedication to the position and the firm, and simple self-discipline. Don't underestimate how hard it is to run a firm on which the sun never sets.

Third, if you think the creative ability of competitive Type A's, working together in a single office, to spontaneously generate tensions where none need exist, to obsess over purely imaginary slights, and to perceive favoritism mysteriously visible only to themself and themself alone, can be challenging, try expanding the canvas to a few continents.

Is the "home office" throwing its weight around? Or are the outposts making irrational demands? Are the practitioners in the most profitable practice areas appropriating more than their "fair share"? Are the practitioners in the least profitable practice areas trying to hold up the firm for ransom? Does the geographic footprint of the firm's offices, always and inevitably a creature more of history and experience than reason and logic, make plausible sense? If not, how far out of kilter is it? Bad enough that it needs to be addressed or just tolerably bad, and tinkering would cause more *sturm und drang* than it would be worth?

This is all to say: We bandy about the term "one-firm firm" fairly promiscuously, but with global players it really has teeth.

I think it's safe to say that a decade or so ago the common wisdom was that there might be dozens and dozens of these firms, and that they represented in some odd combination of prestige and throw-weight the status to which all right-thinking firms should aspire. (Law Land would never get to any place remotely like the Big Four in accounting because of conflicts, if for no other reason.)

Indeed, ten years ago there were only four firms in the world with more than $1-billion in annual revenue, whereas today there are twenty firms that size. But do not expect there to be one hundred (another quintupling) ten years hence.

I realize that the set of large firms (>$1-billion/year) is not exactly congruent with the set of global players; but the correlation is quite high, and the numbers are vivid.

As to why I don't believe we'll see another quintupling in the next decade:

The firms who are global players today have put a great deal of blue water between themselves and any others who aspire to join their ranks; the challenges of creating an enterprise with a presence in every economically important timezone are not to be underestimated.

Finally, these firms by their nature find their primary clientele among multinationals with similar global presence. In case you hadn't noticed, you might want to know that that's become a particularly volatile and perilous sector of the corporate landscape to occupy. Not even the most innovative firms, at the crossroads of technology and business, have an assured future. (If you doubt me, I have just a few words for you: BlackBerry, Dell, Microsoft).

Yet the ranks of the Global Players are well populated with firms of (by and large) tremendously impressive capability. Regular readers of Adam Smith, Esq. know that I am not a doom-sayer about BigLaw in general, and one reason among many that I'm not is simply this: The ability of these firms to marshal, on a dime, a vast, powerful, and targeted array of impeccable talent, backed up by deep resources, across virtually the entire globe,
is awesome to behold.

A complex, globalized economy will always need such services. So perhaps I should half take back what I said: Being a Global Player is no guarantee of success, or even indefinite viability, but if you can play in these leagues you may have some serious fun doing so.

Capital Market Firms

Capital Markets

Next in our typology are the capital-markets centric firms.

These firms are headquartered in a global financial center, often have a history of being tethered to a major bank or investment bank, and enjoy, intrinsically, the most lucrative, high-margin practices. On the downside, they can be run the risk of an attitude of parochialism and conceit, and can be vulnerable to global dislocations and complacency.

If you think this moniker roughly translates to the classic New York white shoe elite, you're right; it's a familiar beast (if not from personal experience for most people, at least from a distance).

But, as much in our world at the start of the 21st Century, it's not exactly that simple. Here's what's different about these firms.

First, recall that we've hypothesized seven primary species: global players capital-markets specialists:

1. Global Players
2. Capital Markets
3. Kings of Their Hill
4. Boutiques

5. Category Killers
6. The Hollow Middle Ground
7. Integrated Focus

My theory is that what's exceptional—indeed unique in our taxonomy—about the capital-markets specialists is

> In an odd way, the greatest threat to these firms may be their own tremendous success.

that the Great Reset mattered less to them than to any other category, and indeed to some of them it only reinforced their ability to go from strength to strength.

If you care to detour with me for a moment into how the Great Reset hit each of our categories, I'd say it hit ##1/global players, 3/kings of their hill, 4/boutiques, and 5/category killers "normally" in our industry, which is to say quite hard. It hit #6/the hollow middle with a couple of torpedoes below the waterline, which is to say very hard indeed, although the damage may not be entirely evident as yet to the naked eye, and #7/integrated focus is the new category emerging largely in response to the Great Reset.

But the Great Reset's impact on our topic du jour, #2? Not bad; maybe even half-good.

Why so?

A result, not the only one but a conspicuous one, of the Great Reset has been a flight to quality coterminous and simultaneous with a flight to value.

I use the terms "flight to quality" and "flight to value" because they're common parlance and everyone knows what you mean when you employ them. But intellectual rigor requires that I specify I really mean "flight to pedigree," or impeccable name brand, where cost is all but irrelevant, vs. "flight to economical," or the world of "good enough is sometimes good enough," where cost is first or almost so on the list of decision criteria.

Lest you think the distinctions between "quality/pedigree" and "value/economical" are overly fussy or fastidious, my point is quite serious: Quality and value can be found at the top, at the bottom, and at all levels of the food chain. But we defer, again, to common usage.

Our capital markets heavyweights represent quality incarnate, so they've come out by and large winners. If you doubt me, look at the AmLaw 2012 results reported so far. Let's use "Value per Lawyer" as our rough and ready proxy, which AmLaw defines as a measure of "how much money, on average, each of a firm's lawyers contributes to overall partner compensation." Let's set aside quibbles about methodology and focus impressionistically on the firms at the top of this particular food chain.

Tell me if you see a pattern:

- Cahill: $730,000
- Cleary: $415,000
- Cravath: $630,000
- Davis Polk: $495,000
- Milbank: $610,000

- Paul Weiss: $540,000
- Simpson Thacher: $590,000
- Sullivan & Cromwell: $755,000
- Wachtell: $1.580-million

If you wonder whether these numbers are impressive or mid-pack, because it's not a familiar metric, here are a few comparables if you'd like (random selection):

- DLA: $235,000
- Baker & McKenzie: $195,000
- SNR Denton: $230,000

Here are a few other AmLaw metrics, this time change in gross revenue in 2012 vs. 2011:

- Paul Weiss: +12.4%
- Wachtell: 11.2%
- Sullivan & Cromwell: 6.4%
- Cravath: 6.2%
- Davis Polk: 4.4%
- Simpson Thacher: 2.0%

In a "growth is dead" market, these are by and large impressive numbers, and Paul Weiss's and Wachtell's are shockingly good. If our pie, as an industry, is relatively static (adjusted for inflation and global GDP growth), it looks as though many of these firms are expanding their market share. They must be doing something right.

So are these firms "golden," having found an incredibly fit-to-purpose sweet spot in the market? Do they have anything to worry about?

As a New Yorker born and raised, I should be the first to cheer them on and wish the answer were no. But I can't say that.

The good news is that these firms are (still) on a roll, and they have been for a long time. The bad news is that New York's share of global capital markets activity has almost certainly peaked, and

> Beware a generational divide between short-term and long-term outlook.

having 85%—100% of your lawyers in Manhattan may not be the one and only real decision you need to make any more in order to thrive.

In an odd way, the greatest threat to these firms may be their own tremendous success. When you're in the highest-rate market, with some of the best-paid partners, serving some of the most prestigious clients in the world, anything you do to broaden your base or diversify can only mean one thing for profits: Dilution.

In other words, almost anything these firms do to un-hedge their bets is self-defeating for at least the next several years. And most partners' time horizons are far shorter than "several years." So even though the Great Reset seems hardly to have mattered to these firms—indeed, may have played to their "flight to quality" strengths—the global tectonic shifts taking place as capital increasingly focuses on the East and the South and less on the West and the North, may mean their fundamental footprints need revisiting. (Ten percent of Harvard Law School students in the class of 2015 are foreign-born.)

To answer the question as to whether or how soon this evolving re-emphasis in the global economy constitutes a meaningful threat to these firms requires looking quite a ways out, and having plausible forecasts about such things as the velocity of globalization, the probability of enduring regional conflicts or intermittent paralysis-by-terrorism, the long-run demographic and sociopolitical trends on various continents, and more.

Since few possess that crystal ball, permit me to suggest where we seem to actually *be* in the market right now. I sense a potential generational divide.

It's not complicated: If I were 55 or 60 years old and a partner in one of these firms, I would instinctively, roundly, and rightly (so far as my own future is concerned) dismiss any of these worries. My effective time horizon is five or ten years, and all should be smooth sailing for at least that long. Reputational markets are extremely sticky, if nothing else.

But if I were 40, with a time horizon of a few decades? Wouldn't I be wondering, "What's the plan here, guys?"

I don't know about you, but that's exactly what I would want to know. The problem is that the answer is far from obvious.

A bigger problem by far—if true of any of these firms—would be if they're not thinking as hard as they possibly can about answering that question.

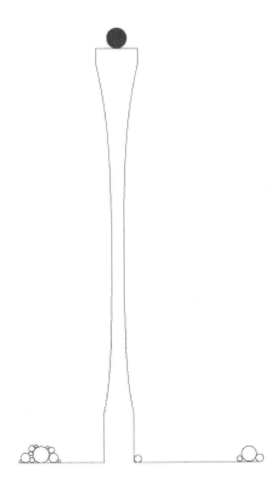

KING OF THEIR HILL

Kings of Their Hill

The label alludes to the children's game (sometimes called "King of the Mountain" or "King of the Castle") whose object is to stay on top of a prominent hill or pile. I obviously use it in the metaphorical sense where a single winner is chosen from among multiple competitors, although there may also be a hierarchy established where others farther down the hill in the pecking order have recognizable roles and statuses.

I must confess that I find this species one of the most challenging to pin down of all seven in our taxonomy: From one perspective they can appear vulnerable to the changes shaking the industry—especially market-empowered clients and the simultaneous flight to quality and flight
to value.

Yet from a more positive perspective you may well conclude they're nicely insulated from the tectonic trends and ought to be secure in their chosen home territories.

I'll elaborate in a moment, but first let me, following Linneaus, simply describe the Kings of Their Hill species. (We'll call them "Kings" for short.) By and large, they are firms:

- headquartered in non-global cities
- cater to desirable upper/middle market clients, mostly non-financial corporations and very high net-worth individuals (the 1%)
- and are solidly embedded in their local markets

During the latter half of the 20th Century, these firms found themselves planted in tremendously fertile soil. But they need to beware two perils: First that their markets may be moving out from under them, and second, that their senior partners who own core client relationships may be falling short on the responsibility to hand down those relationships to a new generation.

There are a host of such firms, and some of them are quite large indeed, ranking comfortably within the AmLaw 50, but in an odd way they are a residual category consisting of firms that don't fit credibly or plausibly anywhere else.

Where did these firms come from and where are they going?

First, where they came from is the easy question: As any thoughtful reader well knows, BigLaw had a golden age from ca. ~1980 until September 2008. That economic environment, *sui generis* in our lifetimes (and absorbing the entire career of some fortunate souls), will never return. In those palmy times, it's no surprise that some favored firms found themselves rooted in fertile ground and grew accordingly. It came with the territory.

Understand what I'm not saying: I'm *not* saying firms couldn't exploit their blessed circumstances more or less effectively, and I'm *not* saying that individuals don't matter. Individual leaders matter, and the only reason we don't think of firms that failed to take advantage of the incoming tide is because, well, they didn't. So they've been passed by and dropped off the radar. Call it survivorship bias, call it tautological, or merely call it *res ipsa loquitur,* but firms that lagged in the tailwind-fueled race aren't big players today.[3]

Now, where are they going?

During the latter half of the 20th Century, these firms found themselves planted in tremendously fertile soil.

This requires balancing the pros and cons of what these firms have going for them.

---

[3] I've talked about "survivorship bias" in various contexts, but it's worth recurring to it here for a moment. It's a sufficiently well-known phenomenon in statistics and financial analysis that it has earned its own Wikipedia entry, which defines it thus:

Survivorship bias is the logical error of concentrating on the people or things that "survived" some process and inadvertently overlooking those that did not because of their lack of visibility. This can lead to false conclusions in several different ways. [...]

Survivorship bias can lead to overly optimistic beliefs because failures are ignored, such as when companies that no longer exist are excluded from analyses of financial performance. It can also lead to the false belief that the successes in a group have some special property, rather than just coincidence.

This is germane to our analysis of King firms because the firms we think of when we think of this category *are the very firms that have benefited from a salubrious geographic home base.* Firms of equivalent sophistication, resources, talent, clientele, etc., who were unlucky enough to plant root in economically challenged metropolitan areas are no longer on our radar.

Pros:

- They have a desirable, upper/upper-middle-market client base—and a base that is not super-aggressive or, frankly, sophisticated, in putting pressure on rates.
- They know themselves, their home turf (if they're regional), what they do and who they do it for.
- Being (by hypothesis) in non-global metropolises, they have a built-in cost advantage.

Cons:

- They'll never work on the biggest, sexiest deals or litigations and will never attract superstars.
- They're in a perpetual battle for market share, with the corollary that they have no choice but to maintain high-caliber talent without pushing their rates into uncompetitive territory.
- For most, their client base is slowly eroding, with no obvious brake handle available.

I said at the beginning that I find this category problematic. Why so?

On the positive side, they can be large fish in what are today attractive ponds; but on the negative side, I'm afraid some of those ponds could dry up.

The real estate bromide is "location, location, location," and I think there's an analogous lesson in that for these firms.

That is to say, I suspect that whether there's an available long-term equilibrium strategy for these firms—who by hypothesis are going to keep their center of gravity where it already is— depends on the economic health and growth prospects of their home territory Over which they have no control.

A few years ago Greg Jordan, then CEO of Reed Smith, was asked at a conference why he decided the firm needed to expand aggressively beyond its historic Pittsburgh base. He replied: "Pittsburgh is a great place to headquarter a sophisticated corporate law firm...if it's 1880."

> "Location, location, location."

Stated differently, their prospects depend on how utterly unforeseeable macroeconomic, regional, and local factors play out. These factors can include:

- Population migration—think of the great Sun Belt gravitational pull of the past 50 years
- Erupting technological centers of gravity (Silicon Valley, Austin,   San Diego)
- University-centric hotbeds
- Business-friendly political environments (Texas, and, I would argue, New York City, at least for the past 20 years)
- Resource riches (Texas again, Calgary and Alberta, Canada)
- And of course the antitheses of all of these.

What all the King firms can pin their hopes on is their clientele being desirable on the one hand and (ironically) unsophisticated about exerting severe market power in terms of rate pressures on the other. Or, alternatively, they can use the intrinsic cost base benefits they enjoy to address pricing pressures.

That can sustain a good long run. But my intuition, and economic history, suggest that the successful firms in this category has been especially blessed by good fortune in choosing their geographic base wisely.

To put it bluntly, relying on that good geographic fortune to continue indefinitely doesn't strike me as an informed and winning long-run bet.

Yet in their defense:

Clients of these firms tend to place great stock in their personal relationships with their lawyers. They think of their lawyers as trusted business counselors, not hired guns picked for a one-off engagement. This does not imply they're indifferent to cost, but neither are they going to micromanage their lawyer. Disaggregation by these clients? Not in our lifetimes.

Clients of these firms tend to place great stock in their personal relationships with their lawyers. They think of their lawyers as trusted business counselors.

In short, barring real incompetence or price-gouging, it's going to be awfully tough for another firm to disrupt these relationships.

Let's look at this a little more deeply. If corporate centric firms face competition, where does it come from? On close analysis, the answer may be less than obvious.

To begin with, clients in the market for another law firm—like people contemplating the purchase of any costly good or service—incur what in econ-speak is called "search costs." And if the client isn't spending such an exorbitant amount on their law firm, there are real intellectual, personal, and (yes) economic reasons to forego the search entirely and stick with the tried and familiar.

Could boutiques offer competition? No matter how nimble they might be, what have they really got to offer these clients?

Capital markets firms or global players? Not exactly: By hypothesis the corporate centric firms predominate in markets the world-class players have chosen to ignore. Not that a Cleary or a Davis Polk *couldn't* dislodge clients from these firms—they probably could—but while a $150,000/year client is very nice indeed to one of our corporate centric firms, is Cleary or Davis Polk really going to bother? Why?

I think the biggest risk to these firms may be internal, not external: A combination of mortality among these firms' senior partners (the ones with the key relationships) and reluctance to effect a client transition to the next generation at the firm.

Two opposing trends are at work, and where you come out on the "generational transfer" issue depends on which you think is stronger.

Both trends are part of a much larger, and altogether different, subject, but what I want to introduce for your reflective moments is whether you believe (a) that the next generation may have a propensity to fumble the baton they're being passed, *or,* (b) that junior partners are actually more willing and able than their seniors to embrace a business-minded client orientation if only given half a chance.

To know where you stand on this, ask yourself which of these sounds more accurate:

- You're worried that you don't see the "holistic" approach we're positing for these senior lawyers being cultivated by many more junior lawyers today. You fear we've gone through a period of recruiting-by-credentialism where we've ignored the client relationship skills which are actually infinitely more important in the long run than GPA and law review. *Or*
- Junior partners have grown up in a world where the business dimension of client relationships has never been more important—both in terms of the lawyers understanding the client's business and the client wanting the lawyer to be a truly close counselor, so they'll grab the baton with alacrity and accelerate.

Finally, there's the issue I raised at the outset of this chapter: The high net worth individuals and tasty private corporations which are the lifeblood of these firms may be slowly moving out from under them. Major Bank A, Big Manufacturer B, Regional Real Estate Developer C, may no longer be what they once were, or they may have been acquired, merged, or simply moved on to larger regional centers (from Phoenix to LA, from Minneapolis to Chicago, from Nashville to Atlanta, etc.)

Their clientele, in other words, may be a perishable and wasting asset. Replacing what's lost, with local acorns that will grow into oaks, is a far dicier and uncertain business challenge, especially in an era characterized, as I believe today's world is, by a battle for market share.

The coming generations in these firms will need to be as talented at capturing the role of trusted legal advisor to new and emerging companies as their forebears were. Moreover, they will need to ensure the firm is structured to provide all the legal expertise the new wave of clients will need, in all the important places they'll need it. (Think of the analogy to a global firm, only one that focuses on owning an economically coherent region.)

Ultimately, King firms may find they need a different gene pool among their professional talent. They may need to transition from lawyers superb at trusted advisor relationships they inherited, to lawyers superb at creating brand-new relationships of equivalent quality who can do things better, faster, and cheaper.

BOUTIQUES

Boutiques

Boutiques are next up, and first a word about what I mean when I say "boutiques," because I may be using it a bit differently than you might assume.

In my nomenclature for purposes of this conceptual mapping, boutiques are firms that do one and really only one thing exceptionally well. They may or may not be small.

This means two things: First, one could conceivably envision a 1,000-lawyer "boutique" (size isn't a criterion), and second, "they do one *and really only one* thing exceptionally well." The "really only one" condition means if you name one of these firms, there will be widespread agreement on what that one thing is—even if they have ancillary practices that may (or may not) exist to serve that primary calling card.

> In industry after industry, boutiques have proven themselves a very durable model.

So what about boutiques?

For starters, they will always be with us. In industry after industry, boutiques have proven themselves a very durable model. Why? Most obviously, boutiques are an evergreen category: Someone or some group is always coming along founding another boutique. Even if the mortality rate is high (more about that anon), the fertility rate is at least as high. After all, the commitment required to launch a law firm is well within reach of thousands of people—hundreds of thousands if you count solo practices.

As we've often observed, law firms are not intrinsically capital intensive, so there goes one potential barrier to entry. Second, in this market in spades, talent is widely available. Vacant office space can always be found even in the tightest of markets, particularly given the tiny footprint boutiques typically launch with. And technology tools are ubiquitous, commoditized, and thanks to Moore's Law faster-better-and-cheaper every year.

Finally, clients are always and everywhere the scarcest commodity, but show me the founder of a boutique who launched without one or more marquee clients and I'll show you a subject for extended psychoanalysis (or an intensive boot camp in Accounting 101 under a CPA with a sadistic streak).

Hence the very high boutique fertility rate, which, importantly, is only enhanced in Law Land because lawyers are autonomy-seeking missiles always prepared to chafe at even the most unjustified feeling of being "managed." Some are walking hair triggers prepared to light out for the territories.

So what are the pros and cons of these creatures?

Pros:

- Vitality and a youthful outlook
- Focus
- Clarity of vision
- Charismatic leadership
- A dream in terms of branding

Cons:

- Limited resources
- Zero or immaterial diversification
- Narrowness of scope, vulnerable to cyclicality in markets

And the management priorities and challenges of boutiques?

- Succession planning
  - Management has to actively, purposefully, and continually cultivate—not just tolerate—next-generation talent
- Rigorously maintaining focus
  - Running a firm that does "really only one thing" requires you to keep saying no
- Maintaining a high level of involvement in the firm
  - Avoiding the cult of personality around the founders and ensuring that everyone feels they're contributing in a meaningful way that's recognized, appreciated, and rewarded
- And did I mention succession planning?

Stepping away from Law Land for a moment (as regular readers know is my wont), boutiques are ubiquitous across the economy, in industry after industry. For example:

- Cars: Ferrari, Lamborghini, Smart, Scion
- Retail: Cartier, farmers' markets, shoe repair, dry-cleaning and copy shops, Etsy

- Apparel: Bottega Veneta, DSquared2, Savile Row, your local thrift store
- Liquor: single malt scotch, "two-buck chuck"
- Hotels: Kimpton Triton, Monaco, and Palomar; "W," Andaz, Morgans, Gansevoort

You get the idea. The study guide takeaways are as follows:

- Boutiques can be high-end or low-end; what's distinctive about them is that they actually ARE DISTINCTIVE and everyone knows it, including, most importantly, clients and potential clients;
- And boutiques—this is non-negotiable, folks—have to stick to their knitting or risk alienating their customers and confusing everyone else.

You may object that boutiques can, and some obviously have, grown into full service firms. Indeed. But that simply means, within our taxonomy, that they're no longer a boutique. (Remember, I stipulated at the outset that firms can migrate between categories.)

I promised to talk about mortality among boutiques.

It's high.

The moment of truth usually comes when the baton needs to be passed from first to second generation management and leadership. It has felled many great and noteworthy firms in the past including Shea & Gould (I was an associate there, albeit not until the very end), Testa Hurwitz, and many more less visible ones.

What goes wrong?

To some extent, it's not boutiques' fault. To be more precise, it's not a failing of the boutique business model; it's a failing of execution and tactics. Boutiques, as we noted, are typically founded by visionaries who are charismatic and electric personalities. They can be a hard act to follow (which is understandable) but they can also subtly or overtly demean, and undermine anyone who might rise up behind them to assume the mantle, which is inexcusable and self-defeating.

> The moment of truth usually comes when the baton needs to be passed from first to second generation management and leadership.

Where does this leave us?

If you're at a boutique, or thinking about going to a boutique, or tempted to start a boutique, ask yourself what Generation Next might look like. If you're young, out of self-interest; or if you're older, out of a sense of stewardship. Be prepared to be excited. Be prepared to relentlessly say No to the wrong things. Celebrate the rare luxury that clients and prospects will know automatically what you're good at. Excel at that thing. Avoid distractions. Stay true to your mission.

And pray for Generation Next.

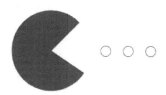

CATEGORY KILLERS

Category Killers

"Category killers" is a term I've borrowed shamelessly from the retail industry. Category killers are firms targeting one broad, but not necessarily high-intrinsic-value, practice. They can be hungry and effective acquirers absorbing any encroachers; the best will persuade other firms to surrender the category entirely.

In retail, these have traditionally been Big Box stores with exhaustive inventory and wickedly competitive prices on one deep "vertical" category of merchandise:

- Home Depot and Lowe's
- Toys 'R Us, Linens 'R Us, ~~Attorneys 'R Us~~
- Bed Bath & Beyond and The Container Store
- Petco and Petland
- Staples and Office Depot

You get the idea. The most salient characteristic of this model is that IT WORKS. If you doubt me, then I have to ask if you disbelieve the famous phrase, "imitation is the sincerest form of flattery," because the concept of category killer retail stores has spread far and wide from its initial roots.

As I use it in Law Land, it means a firm that has the following characteristics:

- Highly specialized in delivering one well-defined practice area and doing it exceptionally well;
- Possessing tremendous depth of resources and expertise in that practice area;

- And able to undercut rivals who only dabble in The Category by investing deeply in processes and management to optimize their service delivery.

> The bottom line is pretty simple:
> You can't beat them at their own game.

This is entirely congruent with what category killer means in retail land. Consider the mapping:

- Highly specialized: When you go to Staples, you're looking for office products; when you go to (say) an employment law firm, you're looking for employment law expertise.
- Depth: If Staples (or staples.com) doesn't have the office product you're looking for, uh, what do you do now? Similarly for our employment law example. If they don't have the arcane expert, who would? You're probably stumped, at least for the moment. (The point isn't whether you'll ultimately be able to find the arcane expertise elsewhere—you doubtless will—the point is that you started with the category killer and will do the same next time, and the next time.)
- Process management: These firms can invest serious resources in optimizing, automating, co-sourcing, templating, and KM'ing best practices, document assembly, and more—and continuously can push work down to lower-cost resources while maintaining or even enhancing quality through exploiting the never-ending learning curve. *This is the secret sauce.*

The bottom line is pretty simple: You can't beat them at their own game.

And you see this in the migration of talent.

I've spent time at several of these firms, and because I'm a curious fellow and genuinely interested, I like to ask people about their backgrounds: "Where did you come from?" "What do you like about what you do?" "Why are you here?" "Tell me about your colleagues."

The answers reveal commonalities:

- Many—I bet most—of them came from other firms, some ostensibly more prestigious, but where they didn't really seem to fit in;
- They love what they do because they're appreciated for it; virtually all of their colleagues do pretty much the same thing, or something highly complementary, and shop talk is natural and seamless;
- And they know that for what they do there's no better place to do it.

Let me go back to the "secret sauce."

Other firms can't afford—and it makes no sense—for them to invest in deep optimization of processes in practice areas that aren't core to their business. category killer firms have one and only one practice area that's *really* core to their business, so the question of how much to invest flips from "what can we afford in this marginal area?" to "how can we **not** invest as much as we can as fast as we can to build insurmountable barriers to entry?" Guess what: They're building insurmountable barriers to entry.

And, as with the migration of talent, you can see it with the erosion of the category killers' targeted practice areas in the rest of the industry. Employment law is probably the poster child example. More and more mainstream firms are cutting back on, de-emphasizing, disinvesting it (choose your euphemism) employment law. (Maybe everyone claims they do boardroom level executive comp packages, but that's no one's bread and butter.)

Don't category killers sound suspiciously like boutiques? Yes, because they are. To be more specific, all category killers are boutiques, but only a tiny subset of boutiques are category killers. I believe they're worth breaking out as a separate type of firm because their business model aspires to largely dominate a significant practice area, whereas more conventional boutiques co-exist side by side by side with competition and have no expectation otherwise.

Symbolically:

Now, do these firms have management challenges? Join the club; all firms do.

Pros of these firms' business model:

- They're the Masters of Branding: it's self-evident what they do, to clients and potential partners and associates
- They can trump competition
- Talent feels valued
- They tend to have few conflicts.

Cons of the model:

- Lack of diversification; subject to cyclical downturns
- Can become complacent
- No cross-pollination of ideas

And the management challenges? A reflection of who they are and what they do:

- The unyielding requirement to remain rigorous about your focus
- Remain uncompromising in talent recruitment— no "bleeding over" into adjacent practice areas
- And most importantly, disciplined, "continuous improvement" [kaizen] in business process optimization.

Can they screw it up? Permit me to editorialize that the capacity of lawyers to be severely developmentally challenged as businesspeople knows no bounds. But if they can hold it all together, it seems to me the pertinent questions are:

Can you fight them on their own turf?

Why would you want to try?

The question for clients is extremely simple: When you need what they offer, "why go anywhere else?"

HOLLOW MIDDLE

The Hollow Middle

The "hollow middle" are generic, one-size-fits-all firms, which aren't a special destination for anything in particular. As you can reliably infer from the very name of the category, I think these firms face particularly awkward and challenging structural problems. Why so? Read on.

Back in college when I was majoring in economics, one of the fields I became fascinated with was that of industrial structure. Antitrust lawyers swim in the sea of industrial structure, whether or not they think of it that way, but "industrial structure" is simply the descriptor for the study of how companies populate the landscape of an industry.

Some industries are natural monopolies, such as regional utilities or, say, the Port of Los Angeles or the O'Hare Airport Authority. Other industries are atomistic, with no sizable players and no meaningful prospect of sizable players (classically, wheat farmers; more currently, artisanal anything). Many industries exhibit increasing returns to scale, which exert a strong gravitational pull towards monopoly or oligopoly (global aircraft manufacturers, pharmaceuticals, railroads and ocean shipping, petroleum, low-cost retailing, mining and extraction).

> Some industries are natural monopolies. Some display textbook perfect competition. Others are "winner take all." But the vast majority follow none of these models.

Other industries (or more precisely markets), particularly in today's hyper-networked world, are "winner take all", or virtually all. They're markets which exhibit "network effects," meaning the more participants there are the more valuable the marketplace is to everyone, and the less valuable rival marketplaces, less densely populated, are. EBay is the obvious example: Everyone wants to sell stuff there because that's where the most buyers are, and likewise everyone wants to buy stuff there because that's where the most sellers are.

But most industries have none of these innate features.

In the absence of powerful intrinsic structural pressures such as those outlined above, what type of structure do industries tend to migrate towards?

Conceptually, there are three structures that matter most in the real world.

Industry Structure #1: Commodification

The first is migration towards players in the no-frills or low-cost niche.

These are industries where customers just want the 4lowest price and don't find any purported or asserted variation in quality plausible. Now, this is always and everywhere the case with true commodities—our classic bushel of wheat or today's gallon of gas—but it's also true *by and large* with goods and services such as:

- groceries at retail;

- generic painkillers and vitamins;
- wiring and cable;
- and virtually the entire family tree of computers, from servers to desktops to laptops and notebooks.

At the margins (hence my "by and large"), even commodities can be differentiated in the eyes of those who are particularly discerning or simply choosy.

Using our four examples, Whole Foods has staked out differentiated territory in delivering groceries at retail; organic brands have done the same within vitamins; high-end audio/video brands in cabling; and, granddaddy of them all, Apple has staked out a one-of-a-kind position in the computer and hand-held device market.

But all of these exceptions remain relatively niche products, with exacting demands on production, distribution and service, and quality control. Perhaps the least appealing aspect of a strategy of attempting to create a niche product in a commodity marketplace is that, even if you can become the exception that succeeds, you know one thing for sure going in: Your market is always going to be small.

Industry Structure #2: High End Dominance

The second structure of note is basically the opposite of the first, namely migration towards the high end.

Here everyone seems to coalesce around the view that a certain pretty high level of quality is the minimum required or you're not even going to put the offering in your consideration set.

We can all stipulate that major surgery for a loved one or close friend is squarely in this category, but there are other slightly less obvious examples as well. One pair of markets that has moved in this direction—for which I give the geniuses at consumer packaged goods companies extraordinary credit—are the markets for razors and for toothpaste.

It used to be that a single blade was state of the art, but today we're approaching the half-dozen blades per razor milestone, with or without battery power, with or without lubricants and emollients, with available handles of luxurious materials, and as for toothpaste, the generic green cavity-preventing variety of yore is almost nowhere to be found, and in its stead we have probably hundreds of variations from all natural to tartar prevention, whitening, baking soda/peroxide, striped, kids', sensitive teeth, and on and on.

A few decades ago, who knew that we needed these things? But need them we clearly do.

We can also cite Apple here, for having singlehandedly positioned the market for MP3 players at the high end.

Indeed, some of you probably did a double-take at the phrase "MP3 players"—I'm referring of course to iPods.

Now, in a way, each of the foregoing markets is simple, even simplistic, when it comes to analysis. At the no-frills end, competitors who can't lower their costs far enough have little choice but to surrender. And at the high end, if you can't deliver superb quality, with a reputation for same, you'll never get out of the gate. Not much more to be said, at least by way of analysis, although shelves of business books have been written on execution in these spaces.

Industry Structure #3: The Hollow Middle

So at last to the hollow middle.

The "hollow middle" industry structure is both widespread in the economy and extremely stable once arrived at.

These are markets where customers' preferences tend to settle into a polarized equilibrium. In other words, they want to go high-end some of the time and low-end some of the time—and when asked why their answer will amount to a more or less articulate variant on "Well, because it all depends."

But the critically important corollary to this is they hardly ever want to go middle-market. The middle seems unappealing to the point of appearing nearly irrational.

Now, I submit—and back in the days when I was wandering the corridors of the economics department at my college it seemed to be amply confirmed—that the hollow middle industry structure has two particularly salient characteristics:

It's extremely widespread throughout the economy; and

Once an industry arrives at this model, it tends to stay there. It's what's called "an equilibrium solution."

The easiest way to understand what a hollow middle structure looks like is to give you some examples.

- **Apparel:** We want fitted suits, shirts, and dresses from name-brand designers or we want a generic polo shirt and jeans or a semi-disposable frock from the Gap, H&M, or Zara.
- **Beer, wine, and liquor:** The craft brew or a Budweiser;
  a waiting-list-only Screaming Predator Napa Cab or the house Chardonnay; a 12-year-old single malt or the well vodka.
- **Cameras:** The "free" one built into our smartphones or a Nikon or Canon digital SLR with half a dozen lenses each worth more than that smartphone.

- **Home entertainment:** Our iPod/smartphone/¬tablet plugged into a pair of sub-$100 speakers or the concert hall-emulating home theater system.
- **Cars:** An Audi, BMW, Mercedes, or Porsche for the experience; or the Accord or Camry, Civic or Corolla, to get us back and forth 99.9999% of the time when we turn the key.

- **Hotels:** A Four Seasons or Ritz-Carlton; or a Courtyard by Marriott. By now you get the idea but one more example, for a reason.
- And lastly, **financial services:** Private banking from US Trust or Blackrock and your own CPA; or the free $200 minimum balance checking account from TD Bank, plus H&R Block online and an e-Trade account.

I left financial services for last because isn't that the closest approximate analogue to legal services?

My own working hypothesis is that law firms are going to find themselves increasing isolated if they don't have a distinctive, credible, and meaningful value proposition.

Firms that do a little bit of everything—"full service"—but which also don't stand for anything in particular are, in our ecological/biological analogy where we began all this, at risk of belonging to an endangered species.

Understand I would take zero satisfaction in being proven right about this category of firms.

But the arguments from economics and, yes, industrial structure, show that markets look with skeptical displeasure on this category. And once clients begin self-selecting their migration paths either up or down the value chain (or both at the same time, more realistically, because "it depends"), there will be less and less oxygen in the middle of them room.

Do these firms have options other than standing astride the railroad tracks of history?

Of course; everyone does.

Understand that every firm's past development path, partnership composition, clientele, and geographic and practice area footprint will determine what course(s) of action are most readily available to it, but at the highest level of abstraction I see four alternatives, other than the dubious one of paralyzed immobility:

> You have four choices:
>
> 1. Continue what you're doing.
>
> 2. Morph into a boutique.
>
> 3. Morph into an integrated focus firm.
>
> 4. Sell.

- Continue doing what you're doing, but with a different mindset, attitude, and approach. I do not jest.

    In management literature, industries or firms that have reached the mature stage of their life-cycles are often deemed wise to adopt an approach called "harvesting." It's not wrongheaded. Not every organization is equal to the task of beating relentlessly upstream, or choosing a self-conscious and purposeful path of moving to a value/price proposition, transforming itself into a different kind of future business. Playing out the hand one is holding can be a rational choice.

There's more: Institutions, as people, have no entitlement to perpetual life. Viewed this way, that a firm might one day cease to exist is no indictment whatsoever. The far more important question is whether during its life it provided valuable client service; a fair and just living and decent treatment to those working there; and a modicum of intellectual adventure and true service to the cause of justice.

Better yet, for those in the firm with retirement in sight, a soft landing is almost guaranteed. The firm isn't going to implode overnight—not unless you do something preposterously wrong (in which case you only have yourself to blame). So: See it through. Recognize the firm is in the September or October of its years, that it had a worthy run enormously beneficial to many who worked and are working there. Choose not to fight history.

- Morph into a boutique. Choose the one core capability you want to be recognized for, and bend all your efforts to investing in that while shedding everything else extraneous to it. Yes, you have permission to keep a few ancillary practices that are nice complements to that One Primary Thing, but make a choice, stick to it, and enforce it. Evaluate every new hire, every financial/IT/marketing decision, every performance review, strictly through the lens of whether it serves that one thing. You may have to break some china along the way, but consider the alternative.

- Aspire to become an integrated focus firm (see our next chapter). This is in many ways an even more rigorous and demanding version the boutique route, but it begins from an external client/market focus rather than an internal personnel/capabilities focus, and (full disclosure) it almost surely entails a higher "beta," as they say
on Wall Street.
Beta, in a word, is risk. More technically, "it is the number measuring the systematic risk of a portfolio based on how returns co-move with the overall market." I use it here to mean that the integrated focus strategy is far likelier than the boutique route to make your firm's performance highs higher and lows lower than that of Law Firm Land in general.

- Merge, sell, or be acquired.

This is the simplest route of all, of course, because in a stroke it essentially makes your problems someone else's—and transforms the very nature of those problems, of course, in the bargain.

The best mergers attack a hollow middle firm's most threatening challenges—lack of daunting scale, no crisp and indisputable "go to" position in the market, vague and amorphous identity—into powerful additions to the platform of a firm that could benefit from additional capacity in areas you would bring to the table.
As for mergers that score somewhat more poorly on the strategic brilliance spectrum, we'll spare you painful exegesis but assume they lack some or all of the benefits above and add in that fairly reliable assumption that they're mishandled in execution, and you get the picture.

A closing note: If you think, or worry, that your firm is in the hollow middle, a word of consolation. In all likelihood, you did nothing wrong. Before the era of "Growth Is Dead," there was no urgency to be otherwise. The rapidly incoming tide solved, and/or hid, a multitude of suboptimal strategic calculations.

But: That was then and this is now.

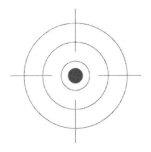

INTEGRATED FOCUS

Integrated Focus

Before we leap into the final category of firms in our taxonomy—"integrated focus"—let's recur to first principles and re-state what we're trying to solve for.

The issue is what do firms do to (in Darwinian order):

- (a) avoid extinction;
- (b) eke out a marginal existence;
- (c) remain relevant;
- (d) continue to perform about as well as before;
- (e) take market share from competitors; and, at the top of the food chain:
- (f) significantly reinvent themselves so as to deliver value to clients heretofore not available.

We may be witnessing this dynamic playing out more quickly in the City of London than we do in the US (at least for now....), with the availability of outside capital in England and Wales accelerating the market's winnowing genius. Just this past week I had breakfast with the former managing partner of an AmLaw 50, who spent a large portion of his time building his US firm's London office, and who observes that the UK market has seen

> "Integrated focus" firms start with an external client/industry orientation, and design the firm around what it takes to serve that market segment superbly.

"a decade's worth of change compressed into three years—and not all of those firms may know how to respond."

Back to: What are we trying to solve for?

I submit that, in this Post Great Reset market, we're trying to create or evolve or reaffirm the essence of each of our firms such that they have a distinctive and recognizable place in the eyes of clients and other critical audiences such as potential laterals. That essence needs to be:

- **credible**—in the fundamental and essential sense that everyone believes your firm can stake a claim to what you're purporting to stake a claim to;
- **distinctive**—meaning not every Susan, Dick, and Harry firm can claim that same position; and
- **beneficial to clients**—meaning it's something they care about and will value, select you for, and pay for.

In Corporate Land, this is often called the brand's "Unique Value Proposition."

Before I hear you scoff at what might strike you as a shallow or simplistic phrase, I have one piece of news and one small thought experiment for you.

The news is that the corporate world—not just in the US but globally—takes this concept very seriously indeed. Firms who know their way around communicating to customers—think Procter & Gamble,

Johnson + Johnson, BMW, Nike, Apple—spend a great deal of time and money crafting the "unique value proposition" for each of their brands. I somehow doubt they're all delusional.

And the thought experiment? Put yourself in the mind of a client trying to narrow a panel roster or choose invitees to an RFP. You have only so much time and mental energy to devote to the task. Which type of firm is more likely to make the cut—the one whose identity is somewhat diffuse and indistinct or the one whose credible, distinctive, and compelling value proposition comes instantly to mind?

Integrated focus firms—whose success is no more guaranteed than that of firms in any other category—at least start from the right place here. Where is that?

They started with an *external* client focus, or more precisely a focus on a particular industry, and design the firm around what it takes to serve that industry (implicitly, that set of clients) superbly. This is the reverse of most firms' approach, of course, who design themselves around what they think some archetype of a Law Firm ought to look like: "Well, we ought to do litigation and corporate, and then some other things as well, probably; we'll figure it out as we go along." I exaggerate, but not much; I've actually heard this "strategy" expressed.

I exaggerate, but not much; I've actually heard this "strategy" expressed.

Now, I'm not going to rehearse the conceptual map I've created to date, but I hope it's clear that I'm skeptical about the half-life of firms in some of the categories. *And it's not because firms in the threatened categories are doing things wrong.* It's both subtler and more menacing than that.

The signal reality of our post-reset world is that clients are increasingly calling the shots. Firms that continue to operate on one or more of the assumptions that

- (a) clients are price-takers;
- (b) cost-plus (the billable hour) has gotten us this far so what's not to like;
- (c) in recruiting associates, pedigree trumps everything else (actually we think we don't even need to know anything else);
- (d) the rich rewards we've been able to deliver to our equity partners heretofore speak for themselves; and/or
- (e) nothing needs to change because you can't argue with decades of success

> Incumbents challenged by disruptive upstarts redouble their focus on serving the same clients the same way; this may be a self-destructive reaction.

If your firm subscribes to much or all of the above, you are going to find the marketplace increasingly hostile.

The way this works out—don't take my word for it—is as devastatingly described and critiqued in Harvard Business School Professor Clayton Christensen's classic *The Innovator's Dilemma.* To wit, incumbents challenged by disruptive upstarts redouble their focus on doing what they know how to do best (meaning serving the same clients the same way only more so) while the upstarts slowly at first but inexorably over sometimes shockingly short timeframes move upmarket until the incumbents' best clients realize they have a clearly superior alternative. Game over.

Let's go back to where we came in here: What are the themes of the law firm taxonomy series?

- The days of one-size-fits-all law firms, if they ever existed, are receding farther and farther into the past. Targeted specialization and deep expertise is more and more the order of the day.
- Clients are increasingly discriminating about what legal services they buy and under what terms, but you'd be mistaken to think it's all about the uni-dimensional element of price. It's about perceived *value*, which is entirely different. We won't here digress into the n-dimensional space of what constitutes value in a client's eyes, but suffice to say there's a lot more to it than price.
- The composition, structure, and (it's not too much to say) essence of most firms is not the result of logic or purpose or intention, but of history, circumstance, and opportunism. Yes, luck may have (and has) shined brightly on many firms, but counting on that to continue as a business strategy going forward is not odds-on a winning hand to play.

So I've found myself asking what a law firm purpose-built to meet specific client needs, and which can simultaneously duck the relentless pricing pressure associated with disruptive innovators and market-empowered clients, would look like.

Not to disappoint you anticlimactically, but the reality of dynamism in markets is that we don't really know. But I have a nominee for a strong potential category type, and yes, it's the "integrated focus."

This type of firm does a few highly complementary things very well—and doesn't do anything else.

For example?:

- Imagine a firm that excels in securities broker-dealer regulation, white collar and governmental investigations, and financial services compliance;
- Or a firm that's a go-to name brand for all things healthcare-related: IP, regulations, insurance, etc.
- Or a firm that does worldwide high-stakes litigation, arbitration, and asset tracing and recovery.

You get the idea.

Are there lots of these firms? No. A better answer might be: Not yet.

Think about this model. What it has going for it:

- Focus
- A clear branding/client benefit message
- High intrinsic profitability

Its challenges:

- Limited capability (by definition); down cycles can hurt
- Have to choose the right clients/industries/specialties
- Partners hoarding clients kneecap the model
- Distributing the spoils (compensation) can be a challenge.

What I like most about "integrated focus" firms is that they seem to me a new species to have emerged recently on the ecological landscape of law firms. Here at Adam Smith, Esq., we celebrate innovation.

Will they have staying power? Who knows, but if they were stocks I'd rate them a buy.

Will other business models emerge? I devoutly hope so. We need the equivalent of a Cambrian Explosion in Law Land.

Finally, what will the industry look like in the future?

To help answer this question, I turned to readers of Adam Smith, Esq. for their opinions, and ran an online survey for several weeks in the summer of 2013.

The results of that survey are our next topic.

Law Firm Taxonomy Survey: The Readers Have Spoken

Nearly 250 readers responded to the survey during the two and a half weeks it was open, and they came from a broad cross-section of firms of all sizes, primarily based in the US, but with a substantial cohort of respondents in the UK. After a quick recap and description of what each of the seven categories of firms is, the questions posed were:

- Please rank the seven models from strongest to weakest.
- Ten years from now, how will the number of firms in each category change (with answers ranging from "there will be none/almost none" to "about the same number" to "a lot more").
- "My firm is a: _____," and "I wish it were a _____."
- What's your degree of confidence in your firm's strategic direction?
- Which are some of the firms that you think fit in each category—and we want you to name names.
- Finally, open-ended comments were available.

So, to the results.

First, we'll simply present the resulting charts and graphs, and then we'll discuss.

10 Years Hence, How Will the Number of Firms Change?

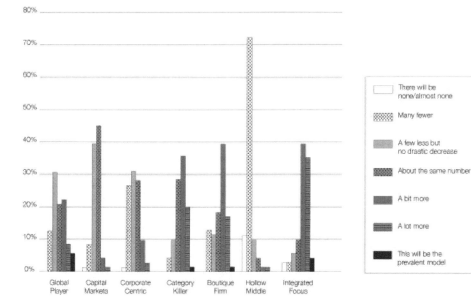

Strongest to Weakest Categories

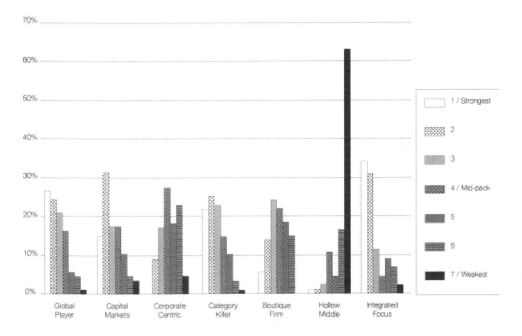

My firm is / I wish it were

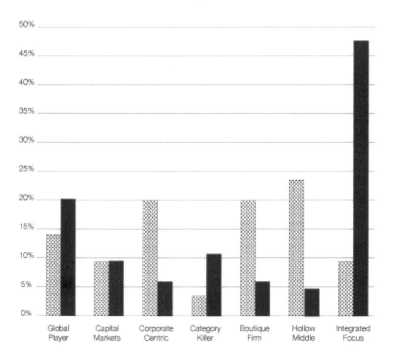

My firm is:

I wish it were:

Your degree of confidence in your firm's strategic direction?

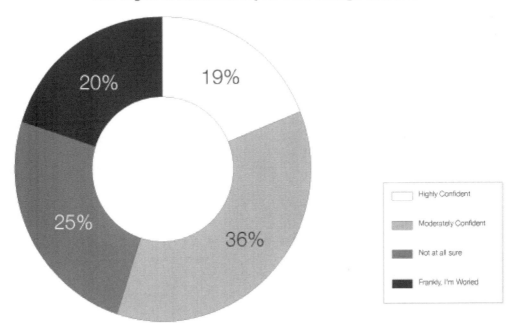

19%

36%

25%

20%

Highly Confident

Moderately Confident

Not at all sure

Frankly, I'm Worried

Discussion

Overall

People seemed to intuitively understand and embrace the taxonomy as an accurate depiction of the BigLaw landscape at the moment—with a caveat.

Strongest categories?
Integrated focus, global player, category killer, capital markets.

Weakest?
Hollow middle, Kings.

The caveat was that several respondents assumed that part of my model is that firms could not have one foot in each of two categories, nor could they be in the process of migrating from one category to another. I intended no such thing, and I would reject both those implied assumptions.

My view is that markets are dynamic, and firms' positions within them are as well. Firms can move both down- and up- market, as well as sideways, and that's a cause for celebration in my book. It means your fate is not pre-ordained, and it means individuals can make a difference.

So what to do with the objection? I choose to reject it. My hunch is that the objection stems from a desire that a classification be a *classification,* with no room for ambiguity. That may have worked for Linnaeus, but not for us.

Strongest to Weakest

Several results stand out here. First, there's quite a horse race among categories deemed "strongest," or the rank immediately next to strongest. Specifically, these four categories all garnered very respectable vote totals on these two categories. (Remember that we're counting votes from two categories so the total allocable by respondents, when converted to percentages, is 200%, not 100%):

- global player: 51%
- capital markets: 46%
- category killer: 47%
- integrated focus: 65%

At the opposite end of the spectrum, it's hollow middle in a runaway (80% combined weakest or next to weakest category), with corporate centric coming in a distant second (28%).

Also interesting was that boutiques were deemed neither particularly strong nor weak, with 66% of respondents ranking them in one of the three mid-pack categories. Only one in 20 ranked them strongest, and nobody at all ranked them weakest. This is powerfully in line with our own view that boutiques are all about execution all the time. The boutique "model" is vibrantly (or promiscuously) open-ended.

10 Years Hence, How Will the Number of Firms Change?

At first blush, one could imagine this is a different way of asking the first question, but I think that's incomplete. I actually believe this question reveals another dimension entirely: Namely, how responsive will firms be to the evolving market dynamics—or can they be?

The results show two outliers: The hollow middle, with 11% nominating it for "none/almost none", an additional 72% voting for "many fewer," and only 6% going for "about the same number" or more. The other is integrated focus, with 74% voting for "a bit or a lot more." The runners-up in combined voting for "a bit or a lot more" was a tie between boutiques and category killers at 56% each.

The message here is clear: Firms that are in the hollow middle *and cannot migrate out of it* are seen as an endangered species, while the appeal of the integrated focus model is great enough that respondents overwhelmingly saw or hoped that firms will be migrating to it.

Is it too late to aspire to being a global player? "Yes: the barriers to entry are almost insuperable." "No: *See*: Norton Rose, DLA."

Interestingly, the most stable category bar none was capital markets: 84% saw the number being about the same or a few less. Here we have a bracing dose of reality: If your firm isn't already there, the barriers to entry—building from scratch a gold-plated reputation in a brutally competitive field where tradition and pedigree count more than anywhere else—are almost insuperable. And the "few less" responses probably reflect another reality: Even if you're in that empyrean, continued incumbency there is by no means assured. It takes decades to build such impeccable brands, and only a few years to destroy them (*see:* Dewey).

Runner-up for "most stable" were global players, where four out of five of respondents foresaw a few more, about the same number, or a few less—in other words, low odds of a drastic change. And I would argue it's for essentially the same reason as the forecast stability of capital markets players: Very high barriers to entry. It's just plain hard to establish a critical mass of capable and well-respected lawyers in virtually every major metropolitan area that matters, worldwide, and even once you may have accomplished that, clients need to believe you're for real.

I hear the back-benchers pointing out that DLA and Norton Rose appear to have pulled off this daunting feat in a few short years—and they would be right to all present appearances—but we don't know whether the Swiss verein model they've adopted to get there has legs for the long run.

At the risk of inciting critics and defenders alike, I'm not here passing ultimate judgment on the verein structure *per se;* I'm just pointing out what seems indisputable to me, that an untested form of alliance which has a track record of only a few years in our industry hasn't demonstrated its long-run hardiness and durability in the face of the inevitable stresses and tensions that will arise.

But since you asked, count me a skeptic. At the very least put me in the Scottish verdict category: "Not proven." These alliances are calculatedly and purposely non-integrated at a basic structural level, and if we've learned anything over the past few years it's that even the most esteemed and *fully integrated* firms are vulnerable to powerful centrifugal forces.

My firm is a/I wish it were a

Strong and consistent results: About 75% of respondents wished there firm were a global player, a category killer or (nearly half) an integrated focus firm. But in terms of what they think their firms actually are, more than two out of three labeled them corporate centric (20%), boutique (20%), or hollow middle (nearly 30%).

In a fascinating and unforeseen result, the only category where "is" and "wish it were" tied precisely was capital markets, at 8% of respondents choosing each. A closer look at the data shows identity between those answering "is" and those answering "wish it were:" In other words, everyone who thinks they're in a capital markets firm is happy to be there, but no one outside a capital markets firm wishes their firm were one. I leave further analysis of this to the psychiatrists.

Confidence in your firm's strategy

Fifty-five percent were "highly" or "moderately" confident, but 25% were unsure and a full 20% chose "frankly, I'm worried." The comments on this provide some real pearls (all of what follows verbatim unless otherwise noted). First, some observations clearly pertaining to each respondent's own firm, but which have far wider resonance:

> Biggest challenge? "We need to overcome the general lawyer's resistance to change. Full stop."

- "Too high a percentage of the business is concentrated in too few clients. Losing the largest of them (we are their primary counsel) would equal at least a 25% reduction in headcount. The result is that we're constantly struggling to meet ridiculous client demands (because they're used to running over us) that other firms wouldn't put up with."
- "Succession planning, succession planning, succession planning."
- "My primary concern is that nothing succeeds like success. My firm has only grown stronger in the last few years, opportunistically poaching key lawyers and practice groups from rivals."
- "The leadership of my firm strongly believes that our clients have issues that are so important or complex that they are fee insensitive. While this may make up a large portion of our work my concern is that the stability in our revenue is driven much more by work that is more mundane and subject to capture by other players."

- *"Of course, the leadership only needs the model to work for the next 5 years; others, like myself, need it to work for 20."* [emphasis supplied]

- "We have shown some willingness to be creative on pricing, but that typically just winds up with clients paying less for what they traditionally paid more for last year. We have not been able to articulate the value of the outputs we can deliver."
- "Despite some real innovation in the marketplace, our internal compensation drivers are still based on one's performance as an individual timekeeper; there are few internal incentives to deliver value or efficiency."

Finally, there are some that display nearly existential angst:

- "We haven't come to grips yet with the need to think about a strategy (more accurately, the lack of a strategy.)"
- "Need to overcome the general lawyer's resistance to change. Full stop."
- "Embracing cognitive dissonance is useful for the practice of law, but should be shunned in developing firm strategy."
- "There is little realization that the 'new normal' has arrived."
- *"Firms that fail to adjust to the external business environment rapidly fail."*

Which firms fits where?

We then asked readers to name one or more firms they thought fit into each category. This generated great interest, with a high percentage of all respondents providing answers. Because the responses were fairly rich, and to minimize noise in the data, we've chosen to list only firms that appeared multiple times in each category.

Let me stress that the following lists were generated from responses to our online survey by readers; they're not what we might think.

Global Players

Allen & Overy
Baker & McKenzie
Clifford Chance
DLA
Freshfields
Hogan Lovells
Jones Day
K&L Gates
Kirkland & Ellis
Latham
Linklaters
Norton Rose
Skadden
Sullivan & Cromwell
White & Case

Capital markets

Cahill Gordon
Cleary
Cravath
Davis Polk
Debevoise
Kirkland & Ellis
Paul Weiss
Simpson Thacher
Slaughter & May
Sullivan & Cromwell
Wachtell

Corporate centric

Akin Gump
Ashurst
Bryan Cave
Dechert
Dorsey & Whitney
Fenwick & West
Foley & Lardner
Fried Frank
Goodwin Procter
Hunton & Williams
Jones Day
King & Spalding
Lowenstein Sandler
McGuire Woods
Morgan Lewis
Morrison & Foerster

Orrick
Paul Hastings
Reed Smith
Shearman & Sterling
Sidley
Squire Patton Boggs
Vinson & Elkins

Category killer

Boies Schiller
Finnegan Henderson
Fragomen
Jackson Lewis
Littler Mendelson
Ogletree Deakins
Quinn Emanuel
Wachtell
Wilson Sonsini

Boutique

Bartlit Beck
Epstein Becker
Finnegan Henderson
Fish & Richardson
Fitzpatrick Cella
Keker Van Nest
Kobre & Kim
Wachtell
Williams & Connolly
Zuckerman Spaeder

Hollow middle

"Anyone in the last 100 of the AmLaw 250"
"Most UK mid-tier firms"
"The rest of us…."

Integrated focus

Boies Schiller
BuckleySandler
Chapman and Cutler
Cooley
Covington
Kirkland & Ellis
Kobre & Kim
Proskauer
Quinn Emanuel
Wachtell
Williams & Connelly
Wilson Sonsini

Additional comments and thoughts

Again, these are reproduced verbatim and any emphasis is mine:

- "As usual, quite thought-provoking. Makes me feel better because identifying challenges is a good first step and I know I have at least some ideas on how to proceed."
- "I think the most fundamental issue preventing firms from changing is how to alter their internal compensation models."
- "There's often a disconnect between a firm's self-perception and the market perception ... For example, [AmLaw 2nd 100 firm] may be able to credibly claim to have a national practice, but it is still clearly a regional firm. In this, I believe that perception is reality because it reflects where potential clients will go shopping for counsel."
- "I think you are spot on. [But] I think even at my hollow middle firm, a few 'known fors' are becoming more prominent. *A big challenge is how to manage that internally when you have have's and have not's.* But the bigger challenge for the majority of firms is how to deliver value to clients when that is at cross purposes with most of our compensation models, which still want to measure [performance] by how many hours are put on a timesheet, and when *the 'market' for our outputs has not yet come into focus.*"
- "You seriously understate a problem that fundamentally faces the business as a whole: The most profitable matters come

disproportionately from clients who have the most sophisticated in house legal advisers, and are thus best positioned to dump outside counsel entirely." [I thought I was speaking to this very issue when I noted that much of the momentum corporate centric firms have enjoyed heretofore has come from their clients' being largely "price takers," but our reader is absolutely right to emphasize the flip side, as it were, that the most lucrative work may be coming from the cohort of corporate clients with the greatest pricing leverage and most sophisticated purchasing systems.—Bruce]

- "Law firms are so insular that it's difficult to determine where to find the best services for a specific issue. Firms that focus on a single [practice] (category killers or IP boutiques) may best solve that problem. However, integrated powerhouses that are one stop shopping for a set of related issues that transcend a specific industry could solve the same problem and provide more balanced revenue flow."

- "However, perhaps the more interesting aspect of this, to me, is the cultural one. Sullivan & Cromwell and Davis Polk occupy very similar niches, but are so culturally different that I can't help but imagine that one might have a materially different future from the other simply due to that element. You've been circling around it for a while, but I'd be interested to hear whether you think that the 'brutal' nature of some of these firms can continue to exist unchanged." [If anything were ever fodder for a different, and very extended, discussion, this reader has nailed it. What an incredibly rich topic on which opinions are sure to violently diverge.—Bruce]

Coda & The Future

Why attempt to compile this guide to law firm business models? Why provide this conceptual map now? Context. Context matters.

People realize the world is changing and they realize that where they start plays a large role in where they can go. That's why thinking in terms of law firm business models—a taxonomy—is helpful and even important.

But what's so special about now? Hasn't BigLaw already reacted to the Great Financial Reset of 2008, in powerful ways, you may be asking?

Let's turn to a discipline far outside of Law Land for an analogy that I believe can give us insight into the broad canvas of our world.

In evolutionary biology, starting in the early 1970's and largely thanks to a paper by the famous Harvard paleontologist and author Stephen Jay Gould, the notion of "punctuated equilibria" posed a serious challenge to the traditional understanding of evolution dating back to Darwin, that evolution proceeded at a relatively constant speed ("phyletic gradualism," to you armchair evolutionary biologists).

The punctuated equilibria theory posits that most species exhibit very little net evolutionary change and are essentially static, but that every once in a while, presumably due to some shock to the ecosystem coming from climate change, a meteor, volcanism, or something else, there are abrupt periods of intense speciation where nature seeks a new macro-level order of creatures and once winners and losers are established, another lengthy period of stasis ensues.

I find this analogy helpful thinking about Law Land today. We have enjoyed a long period of stasis, but now we may be at the start of a period of intense speciation, with new forms of life emerging—some of which will prove adaptive and survive and others of which will be rejected by the antibodies of the marketplace, always vigilant to suboptimal business models.

An important note about what can precipitate spasms of intense speciation in nature: Aside from cataclysmic planet-wide events, a far more common impetus is the sudden invasion of one or more competitive species which have no effective predators in the new environment they're introduced into. Think Asian carp in the Great Lakes, or European rabbits in Australia.

The analogy is simple: The exogenously generated impact on the settled civil practices of the incumbents can be sudden and powerful, and with an outcome that's completely unpredictable—including the triumph and increased potency of the incumbents if they are nimble enough to adapt and reconstitute themselves (on

Seriously upgrading the quality of your professional management will require firms to ostracize lawyers indulging the tiresome and unattractive view that "non-lawyers" are presumably incompetent.

a small scale, what vaccines do to our immune systems).

Let's recap. Here's what has actually been done since the fourth quarter
of 2008:

- Widespread personnel pruning, primarily on the backs of associates and staff and almost never at the expense of partners;
- Managing headcount in far more active ways:
  - summer associate classes are half the size they used to be
  - lateral associate hiring at many firms requires executive committee or managing partner level approval (lateral partner hiring always has)
  - "performance reviews" have often been used as cover for stealth layoffs—this never used to happen.
- Postponing investments where possible, although you can only play this game for so long, and many firms have run out of running room.
- Consolidating office space at any opportunity and slashing "discretionary" expenses, even trivial ones, as symbolic gestures (which often backfires, not least in the heated and utterly disproportionate emotional preoccupation it launches).
- Asking partners—even "non-equity" partners for the first time—to contribute capital, and stiffening capital contribution requirements across the board.

- And so on.

I believe the common denominator across this spectrum of reactions is that they're all directed at preserving the fundamental BigLaw model as we've always known it. Nothing speaks to a serious re-thinking, re-orientation, or re-envisioning of what it means to provide high-end legal services to an increasingly demanding clientele.

In short, we haven't even begun the hard work. We have to get started.

So, again, why this conceptual map? Why now?

To put our degrees of freedom in terms of business models into perspective.

- 20 years ago the concept of global players was maybe on some far-seers' horizon; it wasn't in common parlance;
- Both category killers and, I believe, integrated focus firms are newly identified species on the landscape;
- Corporate centric firms weren't thought of that way; they were simply dominant firms in their region or metropolitan area;
- And, critically and with consequences for how we think about our firms' coordinates on this conceptual map, we know that no business model is bulletproof. Global players can fail (Coudert), as can capital markets firms (Dewey), King firms (Brobeck, Heller, Howrey, Thelen), boutiques (Shea & Gould, Testa Hurwitz), event integrated focus firms (Thacher Proffitt).

The failures are the bad news side of the ledger. The good news side of the ledger is how many new, vibrant, amply populated business models have emerged in the past couple of decades.

If we compile the Law Firm Conceptual Map of 2024 or 2025, I expect it to look so different in key components as to be unrecognizable to players in the industry today. Some of today's populous species, are, I believe, endangered. Other new species not yet imagined will emerge and, Darwinian evolutionary and market forces exerting their inexorable power as they always have and will, the new species will be stronger, more competitive, more structurally "fit."

I understand that never has there been less forward visibility; never has the future seemed as shrouded in fog and noise; never has it seemed more challenging to grab the wheel and set a purposeful course.

I nonetheless venture to believe that certain systemic conditions that will have a powerful impact on shaping the future of BigLaw are already in place, including demand volatility, excess capacity, clients ever more sophisticated about purchasing legal services, and new market entrants.

Their implications are not entirely mysterious:

- Migration towards the high end (the "flight to quality") *and* towards the value sector will accelerate. Firms at the very top of the prestige charts will thrive and claim greater market share, as will those who deploy technology in a savvy way to deliver high-reliability, high-consistency, commoditized work in volume. The middle will be increasingly hollow.

- For most but not all firms, geographic expansion will continue, shoulder to shoulder with the globalizing tropism of our clients. Only a few single-city powerhouses will be at liberty to ignore expansion.

- Will there remain room for intensely focused firms with intimate knowledge of their home territory who excel at a handful of things that clients value? Always. But being able to coast on a reputation as a friendly but less than impressively accomplished local hero may be a less and less viable strategy.

- Firms that choose to excel will for the first time need to get serious about—and will be distinctive in the marketplace for—recruiting, rewarding, and empowering professional management. This will also require those firms to impose strict cultural ostracism on any lawyers indulging the tiresome, juvenile, and frankly repulsive view that non-lawyers are to be looked down upon.

- Parallel to and congruent with increasing the quality of talented professionals in management will be broader and more rigorous capabilities in management. Those new or expanded capabilities will include project management as "standard operating procedure," as well as more rigorous attention to capital structure and balance sheet issues. Slower growth puts a high risk premium on assuming that enough cash will always be coming in the door to cover up slack, and banks will show greater reluctance to lend to law firms and demand higher margins to do so. Finally, law firms will be well advised to invest in more sophisticated risk management, with its associated systems and controls.

- The way firms deploy technology will shift from an emphasis on increasing the efficiency with which lawyers can do what they've always done—"digitizing the quill pen," as a friend accurately jokes— to true innovation in areas including big data, pattern recognition systems, and predictive intelligence. Some of this will threaten to displace the jobs of human beings now doing that very work.

- The path of the early years of a lawyer's career will change, as clients' unwillingness to pay for on-the-job training will force a realignment of the economics and professional development model of junior associates.

  The two- to four-year transition from law student to valuable and contributing practitioner will morph from a cliff to a ramp, with increasingly formal apprenticeship and "residency" programs occupying the transitional years. This will redound to the tremendous benefit of clients, firms, and the human beings involved.

- And at long last, we will move away from our one-dimensional obsession on recruiting those with the top grades from the top schools, because it has consistently failed to produce high-quality, satisfied, long-lasting hires. What it produces instead is simple: Mistakes. At enormous expense.

We will finally adopt some of the same proven psychological and compatibility assessment tools the Fortune 500 and FTSE 1000 have been using for decades—because they work, and because the days of being able to afford profligate waste, surplusage, attrition, and upheaval are gone. (Should I mention we'll widen the net we cast for talent in the bargain?)

- To summarize these changes: The marketplace will continue to grow increasingly competitive, as we shift from "a rising tide lifts all firms" to a fight for market share. The battle will be fought both with traditional law firms subscribing to the imperative of continuously upping their own game, but also with new forms of rivals entering our backyards with types of legal services, delivery systems, and pricing structures that are in some ways substitutes for BigLaw.

  The unmistakable implication is that firms that intend to survive and thrive will need to place an increasing premium on differentiation, in ways that are (a) credible; (b) distinctive; and (c) provide undeniable value to clients.

Uncomfortable and disconcerting and alien to us as all this may be, a few closing words.
That we must change is not a choice. On our side is that we do have resources and capabilities; we're not defenseless.

Those individuals leading law firms today, and their immediate generational successors, will invent our industry's future—or someone else will do it for and to us.

Your firm can unite as one, or not. The challenges we face will require deploying intellect, which is a given, but vastly more important now will be showing character.

To lead, you must:

- *Utterly* reject skepticism, preposterous nit-picking, and factitious fault-finding.
- Denounce and publicly condemn "smartest guy in the room" syndrome; banish those who indulge in it.
- Be resolute in the face of the unknown.
- Find opportunity in difficulties, not difficulty in opportunities.
- Be courageous and resilient with the untried.
- Innovate, for a change.

Face forward, not backward.

The future belongs exclusively to those who do.

Conceptual Map Summarized

Conceptual Map (I)

Model	Comments
Truly global players spanning three or more continents	Top of the food chain predators (but like predators, limited in number)
Capital-markets or M&A centric specialty firms headquartered in a global financial center — often historically tethered to a major I-bank	Intrinsically the most lucrative, high-margin practices, but also prone to parochialism and conceit. Vulnerable to global dislocations, complacency
Kings of their Hill firms headquartered in non-global cities catering to desirable upper/middle market, mostly non-financial corporations and very high net worth individuals	Fertile soil for tremendous growth in the 20th-C.. But these firms need to beware markets moving out from under them

Conceptual Map (II)

Model	Comments
Boutiques: Firms still true to their founding vision and focused on one primary practice area; may or may not be small	Will always be with us; a very durable model
"Category Killer:" Specialists targeting one broad but not necessarily high intrinsic value practice	Hungry and effective acquirers absorbing any encroachers
The Hollow Middle: One-size-fits-all, not a special destination. generic law firms	Endangered, at risk of marginalization, steady loss of high-value practices
Integrated Focus	A fascinating evolutionary innovation

Global Players

Pros	Cons
Presence everywhere matters	Marginal offices with continuing churn
Have created their own barrier to entry	Risk of pachyderm-lack of responsiveness
Comprehensive practice area offerings — diversification as a hedge	Particular sectors suffer cycles of flaccid demand
Areas of very high intrinsic profitability	Obverse; a compensation challenge

Management Priorities
Try to remain nimble in maintaining an economically germane geographic footprint and practice area mix
Stay on top of enormous managerial complexity and overhead
Fight lack of true partnership culture; build firm-first behavior

Capital Markets

Pros	Cons
Sky-high margins come with the territory	Almost any expansion — practice area or geographic — will dilute profits
Typically can rely on at least one deeply institutionalized I-bank client	No relationship, inherited or otherwise, can be taken for granted
Impeccable blue-chip brand name	If it's not bet-the-company work, rates border on punitive
Top of the market compensation	Equity must be controlled with an iron fist; compensation from integrated focus

Management Priorities
Stay bonded at the hip to core I-bank relationships while growing new ones
Talent, talent, talent

King of the Hill

Pros	Cons
Desirable, solid upper/middle-market client base — one not super-aggressive in putting pressure on rates	Will rarely work on the biggest, sexiest deals or litigations; superstars pose a flight risk
Know themselves — what they do and who they do it for	Perpetual market share battle; continual struggle to maintain high-caliber talent without pushing rates into uncompetitive territory
Built-in cost advantage because not in global financial centers	Eroding client base, with no obvious end in sight

Management Priorities
Stay really really close to clients
Avoid the Hollow Middle — migrate towards integrated focus
Query: Is the category itself on the way to becoming a null set?

Boutiques

Pros	Cons
Vitality, youthful outlook	Limited resources
Focus	Zero diversification
Clear vision	Narrowness of scope, vulnerable to cycles
Charismatic leadership	Creation of steerage class?

Management Priorities
Succession planning; cultivate — don't just allow — next-generation talent to thrive
Rigorously maintain focus: must keep saying "no"
Maintain a high level of involvement in the firm and, yes a sense of fun

The Hollow Middle

Pros	Cons
Have been around for a while	Coasting
Do a bit of everything/full-service	Don't stand for anything in particular: a branding nightmare

Management Priorities
Articulate a value proposition that is (a) distinctive; (b) credible; and (c) meaningful to clients and prospects
Focus relentlessly on more disciplined business processes to maintain client base through greater efficiencies
Alternative: Slowly disinvest, harvesting maximum cash profits for today while planning to gracefully shrink
Alternative: Create a path to Integrated Focus

Integrated Focus

Pros	Cons
Focused	Limited capability, down cycles can hurt
Offer a clear value proposition to clients in their target zone	Have to choose the right clients/industries/specialties
Overlapping and complimentary practice areas	Partners hoarding clients disable the model
Very high intrinsic profitability	Distributing the spoils (compensation) can be a challenge

Management Priorities
Perhaps of all the models, the highest maintenance talent pool
Anticipate and respond to macroeconomic changes that could undercut the firm's core offerings

About the Author

Bruce MacEwen

A lawyer and consultant to law firms on strategic and economic issues, Bruce is President of "Adam Smith, Esq." (AdamSmithEsq.com), an online publication providing insights on the business and economic issues facing law firms. Adam Smith, Esq. is also an industry-leading management consultancy to law firms and the legal industry around the globe:

The firm's site has a worldwide readership, with over a decade of archived articles on strategy, leadership, globalization, M&A, finance, compensation, cultural considerations, and partnership structures—totaling about 7,000 pages in print form.

In early 2013 Bruce published the book "Growth Is Dead: Now What?," outlining the consequences for the legal industry of the great financial reset of 2008, which Bloomberg Law immediately called "must-reading, from the one and only Bruce MacEwen."

Bruce and his partner in Adam Smith, Esq., Janet Stanton, are also the co-founders of JD Match, the online legal recruiting platform for the 21st Century. Among other things, JD Match employs a sophisticated algorithm (patent pending) to match the preferences of firms for law students and law students with firms, and a wealth of actionable information not available anywhere else, including a trait assessment tool purpose-built for lawyers.

Bruce has written for or been quoted in: The New York Times; The Wall Street Journal; Fortune, Bloomberg; The American Lawyer, and other publications too numerous to mention. He is a sought-after speaker and frequently appears at law firm retreats and legal industry conferences around the world.

Previously, Bruce:
Practiced litigation and corporate law with Shea & Gould and with Breed, Abbott & Morgan in New York; and Practiced securities law in-house for nearly ten years at Morgan Stanley/Dean Witter on Wall Street.
Bruce was educated at Princeton University (BA magna cum laude in economics) and at Stanford Law School (JD). A native Manhattanite, he lives on New York's Upper West Side with his wife and their dog.

Presentations on the Taxonomy

Adam Smith, Esq. offers presentations and interactive discussions about the topics and themes surrounding the taxonomy to law firms, corporate law departments, and other participants in the legal sector of the economy.

For further information,
please contact Bruce at +1.212.866.4800 or
bruce@adamsmithesq.com.